Sabrina Brightstar
Flow
Forward

**Flow Forward**

**Soul Business Series - Book 2**

Hello Beautiful Souls

I am thrilled you are here. By stepping into this journey, you are saying yes to your highest excitement, to what makes your heart sing. As Bashar teaches, if you feel a desire within you, it is because someone is waiting to receive the benefit of what you create. No idea is meaningless. Your inspiration is evidence that your creation is already wanted.

Open yourself. Trust yourself. Let your gifts flow through you.

I am proud of you. Building a soul aligned business is a sacred path, a spiral of expansion and contraction, clarity and mystery. Through it all, play. Be curious. Let joy lead the way. My soul sings knowing we are creating new frequencies together, rewriting what business can feel like.

We are co-creating in the Field, a space of expansion, beauty, and possibility.

Thank you for being here. Thank you for choosing to Flow Forward.

In delight,
Sabrina

## Table of Contents

# Chapter One: The Experiment Mindset

Many people dream of being their own boss. They imagine the freedom of creating something meaningful, doing work that feels like them, and earning income in a way that feels natural and alive. That desire to be an entrepreneur is powerful. It is the call of the soul to express, contribute, and create. Yet for most, the dream stops before it ever begins. The moment inspiration strikes, fear follows. The mind starts racing with all the things it believes you must know before you start. You tell yourself you should understand taxes, accounting, marketing, design, pricing, websites, social media, and branding before you even dare to begin. You imagine needing a perfect plan, the right name, and the ideal launch before you can take your first step. The vision that once felt thrilling suddenly feels impossible. The excitement collapses under the pressure of perfection, and the idea gets filed away for “someday.” But someday never comes, because that is too much weight for one person to carry before they even begin. This book will teach you the bit-size entrepreneurial model, a way to start small, stay curious, and build confidence through experience rather than overwhelm.

You do not have to start your business as an expert. You begin as an explorer, a curious soul who is willing to see if an idea feels like a match. You are allowed to learn as you go. You are allowed to make mistakes. You are allowed to discover that you love some parts and dislike others. That is how you learn what truly aligns with your energy. The purpose of beginning is not to prove your worth or professionalism. It is to discover what feels alive when you bring an idea into form.

Flow Forward is about recognizing the flow. It is about allowing the cooperative components of your idea, your energy, and the people around you to interact and engage. Every project you create has its own consciousness. It has a unique rhythm, timing, and expression. When you enter a flow-based relationship with your business, you begin to see that it has a personality of its own. It responds to your attention, your emotions, and your belief in its value. Flow is not control forward. Flow is open and generous. It makes room for surprises, twists, and turns. It is spacious enough for detours and discoveries. It asks you to dance, not demand.

The mind wants to manage everything. Flow wants to collaborate. Flow Forward invites you to build a relationship with your project as a living being, not as a checklist to conquer. The more you trust that the consciousness of your business knows how to unfold, the easier it becomes to release control and allow its natural current to carry you.

I have started and failed at many businesses in my life, yet I never looked at any of them as failures. I saw each one as an investment in myself and my learning. I did not pay a business school thousands of dollars to understand entrepreneurship. I invested my time, creativity, and passion in real-world projects that taught me more than any classroom could. Each venture became its own education. I learned by doing. I learned by trying. I learned by listening to what worked and what did not. None of my businesses unfolded the way I expected. You cannot know what something will become until you try.

Some ideas I thought would be easy turned out to be a clear no. Others that began as simple side projects became lifelong skills that surprised me. There were things I thought I would love that I quickly realized were not enjoyable. There were parts of the process I never expected to like, yet they captured my curiosity and led me to new passions. Each business adventure showed me more about myself. Every single one, whether short or long, gave me valuable information about how I work best, what I love, and where I thrive.

The journey of entrepreneurship is a never-ending twist and turn. You will learn who you are in ways that surprise you. You will develop abilities you did not know you had. You will refine your intuition and strengthen your self-trust. It is all on-the-job training. Every attempt becomes a stepping stone toward mastery.

One of my favorite examples from my own life came when I discovered how to use astrology and artificial intelligence together to help people identify their purpose and mission for this incarnation. I was dazzled by how accurate and easy it was. It lit up something inside me. I felt certain I had found my next calling. I imagined becoming a deep and powerful astrology reader, using AI to discover meaningful insights within minutes. I was even considering enrolling in Debra Silverman's astrology school because I believed this was going to be my highest excitement path. My inner being gifted me with a brilliant idea. Before investing in a website, training, branding, or committing myself to a full business, I decided to beta test it. I offered free "What Is My Purpose?" readings for one week. It was a hit. People love free readings. I gave myself a two week window to send everyone a written reading.

It was fun, and it quickly lost its appeal. I had thought this was going to be my next career. Instead, I discovered very fast that daily personal readings were not a match for my design or my joy. I honored my commitment and delivered every reading I promised. As I moved through the process, I realized that what I truly loved was creating systems. I loved discovering shortcuts and tools that others could use. I realized that my best alignment as a Projector was not doing the readings myself but teaching others how to do it. So I wrote an e-book that teaches people how to do their own "What Is My Purpose?" astrology reading using their birth chart and AI support. That was the better fit for my excitement and energy. The beta testing experience gave me the clarity I needed. Without that short, low-risk experiment, I might have invested months or years into something that was not aligned for me. That is the power of sample size entrepreneurship. It lets you gather real data without losing yourself. The e-book is called What Is Your Purpose Your Mission Is Written in the Stars, and it is available on my website SabrinaBrightstar.com.

This is why I teach the bit-size business model. Instead of trying to build a complete company from the start, you create a small, simple experiment. Think of it as a business sample. You are testing the waters to see if the idea brings you joy, if you enjoy providing the service, and if people respond to it. This approach removes the heaviness, the seriousness, and the fear of failure. You can explore your creativity in a way that is easy to try, easy to start, and easy to adjust.

When you approach your business as a bit-size experiment, you take away the high stakes. You do not need investors or a massive budget. You do not need to quit your job or commit for life. You are simply giving your idea a chance to breathe. It is not a forever plan. It is a friendly test. It is a practice in courage and curiosity.

The truth is that most people do not know what kind of work truly lights them up until they begin. They may think they will love making candles, coaching clients, building furniture, or baking pies, but the real clarity only comes from experience. A small project lets you feel what it is like to interact with customers, deliver your service, receive feedback, and witness how it affects others. The only goal is to gather data.

This is entrepreneurship without overwhelm. You can call it a pilot project, a micro venture, or a seasonal gig. I call it a bit-size business because it is small enough to taste, safe enough to test, and flexible enough to change. You are not trying to find your forever thing. You are learning what flows and what does not.

This new way of exploring entrepreneurship is built on curiosity, not commitment. You get to start before you feel ready and let the experience teach you. Instead of overthinking, you observe. Instead of forcing, you feel. You might walk three dogs a week, bake pies for a month, offer a Reiki series, or do a handyman special for five homes. These small projects help you practice real business skills such as creating offers, setting prices, handling clients, and managing time without being crushed by expectation.

The energy shifts from “I must succeed” to “I am here to explore.” That shift opens the door to flow. When you remove the expectation of perfection, you create space for discovery. Each bit-size project builds confidence, teaches you something new, and shows you how to follow what feels alive.

You might find that the thing you thought would be your career becomes a side hobby, and the thing you began playfully becomes your next breakthrough. That is the beauty of flow. It rearranges everything once you step into it.

Flow Forward means you stop trying to control outcomes and start allowing the natural rhythm of life to guide your business. It means you trust that the right people, ideas, and opportunities will converge at the right time. The universe loves to orchestrate cooperation when you are in motion.

You do not have to know how it will all unfold. You do not need to predict, plan, or pressure. You only have to begin lightly and allow the experience to unfold. Flow Forward reminds you that clarity comes from connection, not control. Success grows from motion, not management.

Give yourself permission to start small, keep it simple, and make it enjoyable. Let your project be a test, an experiment, and a conversation with the universe. You are not just building a business. You are building a relationship with your own creative flow.

That is the essence of the Experiment Mindset and the invitation of Flow Forward.

# Chapter Two: Start With One Simple Offer

When people take their idea and shrink it down to a small, friendly experiment, everything starts to move. The fear softens, the mind relaxes, and the energy opens. The magic is not in creating a massive plan. The magic is in the beginning. This is how flow works. The moment you move, energy responds. The Law of Momentum begins to activate.

The Law of Momentum is simple yet powerful. Whatever is in motion tends to stay in motion. Whatever is stuck tends to stay stuck. When you feel trapped, overwhelmed, or frozen in indecision, that energy expands. The mind builds more stories about why it is too soon or too hard. But when you take even one small action, you begin to shift the current. Movement, no matter how tiny, invites cooperation. The universe begins to meet you with support.

This chapter is about creating that first bit of movement. You are going to design your first bit-size business project. Not a full company, not a lifelong commitment, but a simple, joyful experiment that lets you explore what it feels like to offer something to the world.

A bit-size business project is like a science experiment. You are gathering data about yourself, your offer, your clients, and your energy. The goal is not to make it perfect. The goal is to learn.

A small project removes the pressure of trying to get everything right. It gives you permission to Play Your Way to Clarity. You are not locking yourself into a career path. You are simply giving your inspiration a place to land.

When you think of your business as an experiment, you open the door to discovery. You might learn that you love working with clients but dislike scheduling. You might realize that you enjoy creating but not managing. You might discover that the idea you thought was your dream actually leads you to something even better.

A small project gives you real-life experience without the heaviness of a long-term plan. It lets you move forward without risking your peace or your savings.

One of my favorite examples happened over 25 years ago. One of the massage therapists working for me had taken a Reiki training class and felt inspired to offer it, but she did not know how to introduce energy work to clients. At that time, Reiki was not widely known. In fact, many people felt nervous about energy healing. It was unfamiliar and therefore uncomfortable.

We created a small, simple test. We offered clients a complimentary Reiki session at the end of their massage. The therapist took about five minutes before the massage to explain what Reiki was, while reassuring them that they did not need to do anything. Their only job was to relax and receive. It was a 75-minute package with a free 10 minute sample of Reiki included.

This was a true bit-size business experiment. It allowed the therapist to test the idea with zero pressure. She quickly discovered how to explain Reiki to someone who had no experience with energy work. She got real feedback. She watched clients wake up from the session amazed by the deep peace they felt and curious to learn more. She learned what worked in her explanation and what did not. She learned how to hold space for a new experience.

She loved it. Clients loved it. And because of that, we added Reiki as a permanent offering on our menu. I created a Massage and Reiki Combo Package, a 90-minute offering that included 20 to 30 minutes of Reiki as part of the treatment. It became a successful service. We helped people understand energy work in a simple, accessible way, and she built a growing list of clients who benefitted from the offering.

None of that would have happened without one small, low-risk experiment.

Choosing One Idea

To begin, choose one idea that excites you. It should feel alive in your body, not heavy in your mind. The key is curiosity, not certainty.

You might already have several ideas swirling. Maybe you want to try closet organizing for busy families or people preparing to move. Perhaps you feel inspired to become a theme party planner, helping others celebrate birthdays, holidays, or milestones. You might explore being a car detailer, transforming vehicles into spaces that feel clean and new. Maybe you love style and want to become a personal shopper, helping others choose clothes that reflect who they are. Or perhaps you are drawn to something like pet grooming, event photography, meal prep services, or energy alignment consultations.

Do not overthink it. You are not choosing forever. You are choosing for now. Pick one idea that feels light enough to try.

When people get stuck at this step, it is because they try to solve every problem before they start. The mind wants to figure out pricing, competition, marketing, and branding before a single client exists. Let that go. You are not solving business puzzles. You are exploring possibilities.

Ask yourself:
What idea keeps circling back to me
What could I try in the next few weeks without making it complicated
What feels easy enough to begin even if it is not perfect

That is your starting point.

## The Power of a Sample

A bit-size business project is a small-scale version of your idea. It is a way to test your offer in real life. You might offer your service for one weekend, one week, or one month. You might sell a handful of products instead of filling an entire inventory. You might help a few clients instead of building a full schedule.

Keeping it small removes fear because you are not making a life-long commitment. You are simply experimenting.

## Letting It Be Imperfect

A small project bypasses the belief that everything must be ready before you begin. You do not need a polished logo, a fancy website, business cards, or branding. You only need a clear and simple offer that feels fun to deliver, something you can describe in a sentence or two, and something you can begin sharing now.

Let it be imperfect. You can refine as you go. Flow does not require perfection. It simply requires participation.

## Setting a Time Frame

Choose a short window. Short projects give fast feedback and fresh energy. When the experiment ends, you decide whether to continue, to change directions, or to complete it and celebrate the clarity you gained.

## Naming Your Experiment

If it feels fun, give your project a temporary name. It helps give the idea form and personality. It is not forever. It is simply a way to help the energy take shape.

## The Energy of a Sample

When you treat your business as a sample, you shift from proving to exploring. People feel your ease. They sense that you are offering something genuine and joyful. This alignment matters more than any strategy. Energy speaks louder than marketing. When you are relaxed and curious, opportunities find you.

You are never waiting for clarity. Clarity arrives because you moved.

## The Vibrational Practice

Before you start, take a quiet moment to align with your intention. Ask why this idea feels exciting. Each time you work on your project, pause and feel what feels easy. What wants to move. Where you might be trying to control something that does not need controlling.

Your awareness becomes your compass.

Starting a business does not have to be a huge commitment. It can be a living, breathing conversation with life. The more you practice the bit-size business model, the easier it becomes to experiment, adapt, and grow.

Each project teaches you something. Each experience builds self-trust. You begin to realize you are not learning how to start a business. You are learning how to stay in flow.

That is the Law of Momentum at work. When you move, life moves with you.

Choose your idea. Create one small offer. Begin lightly and let the experience reveal what wants to unfold.

That is how you Flow Forward.

# Chapter Three: Protect Your Energy When You Begin

When you begin something new, especially something connected to your dreams, it is normal to feel both excitement and fear. The heart says yes, while the nervous system quietly asks, “Is it safe?” This is why the beginning matters so much. Not the strategies or the branding or the perfect plan. What matters is that you feel safe enough to stay in motion.

Many entrepreneurs lose momentum before they even start, not because they lack passion or talent, but because something inside them tightens. The body experiences change as a risk. Even positive change can feel threatening when it pushes you into unfamiliar territory. And when the body senses risk, it does what it is designed to do. It protects you.

Protection can look like procrastination.
It can look like overthinking.
It can look like perfectionism.
It can even look like suddenly losing motivation for the very thing you were excited about.

This is why so many people feel confused when inspiration disappears. They blame themselves, when actually, their body is doing its job.

Trying something new invites visibility. And visibility wakes up vulnerability. The fear is rarely about the project itself. The fear is about how others might see you. What they might think. What they might say. Whether they will accept your new direction. The nervous system does not separate the fear of being judged from the fear of being unsafe. It interprets both as danger.

If you do not understand this, you might think your stuckness means you are not ready. You might assume your hesitation means something is wrong with you. But there is nothing wrong. Your inner safety system simply needs reassurance.

This might explain why you can feel blocked or start unintentionally self-sabotaging. If you are unaware that your body is trying to protect you, you might misinterpret your own survival patterns as lack of discipline or lack of desire. In reality, you are deeply committed to staying alive and belonging. Your body wants to help you avoid rejection or overwhelm. When you lovingly acknowledge that instinct, you unlock your ability to move again.

Imagine you have a calling to write a book. You feel inspired, clear, and excited. The first pages pour through you. Then suddenly, the enthusiasm fades. You stop writing. You cannot seem to maintain your momentum or your schedule. The voice in your head whispers that you are lazy or unreliable. But none of that is true. Your expansion triggered a protective pause. Your body is not against you. It is asking for reassurance that this change is safe.

You can speak kindly to your body. You can say, "We are safe to try. We are allowed to grow. We can go gently." When you bring comfort to the places that feel afraid, your momentum returns. Your body relaxes into possibility again.

This is why the bit-size business model works so well. It honors your nervous system. It creates a path where the stakes are low and the safety is high. You do not have to quit your job or announce your dreams to the world. You do not have to tell your family or get their approval. You do not have to restructure your entire life to explore one idea.

You are simply giving your creativity a soft place to land.

There was a woman in an online metaphysical community who wanted to explore coaching. She did not feel ready to share her dream with her family. She sensed they would worry or question her. So she kept it simple. She offered a quiet experiment: three coaching sessions, once a week, for three weeks. She shared her offer only inside her supportive online community where she already felt safe. People said yes. She completed her first sample project without turning her whole life upside down. She protected her peace while testing her purpose.

That is the power of starting small. You do not need permission or perfection. You only need one simple offer in a space where you feel supported.

Protecting your energy is not about hiding. It is about nurturing what is new. It is about letting your inspiration grow roots before you expose it to too many opinions or expectations. It is easier to stay in flow when you are not battling resistance from the people around you who may fear change. Their doubt does not mean your dream is wrong. It often means they worry about how change will affect their comfort.

You can keep exploring while they catch up later.

Your only job in the beginning is to reduce the pressure and increase the safety. Keep the project small. Keep the circle of visibility gentle. Keep reminding yourself that you are learning, you are growing, and you are allowed to take your time.

Bit size entrepreneurship protects your heart. It protects your confidence. It protects your belief in what is possible. By moving step by step, you build trust with yourself. You teach your nervous system that you can take action and remain safe.

When safety and curiosity walk together, momentum becomes natural.

This is how you Flow Forward.

# Chapter Four: The Energy of Pricing

Pricing is one of the most emotional parts of entrepreneurship. It touches money, value, identity, confidence, and self-trust all at once. It is easy to think pricing is only a business decision or a strategy, but it goes much deeper than that. Pricing is a relationship. It reflects how supported you feel, how much capacity you have, and how safe you feel being paid for what you offer.

When you are first beginning, pricing can feel especially vulnerable. You might wonder if anyone will think your offer is worth paying for. You might worry people will question the price. You might feel pressure to prove that your idea has value. The number you choose is not just a number. It is a message you are sending to yourself and to the world: this matters. What I give has meaning. I deserve to be supported for the energy I invest.

Pricing brings up emotions because it brings up visibility. When money enters the conversation, your work becomes real. You are declaring that what you do has value. That level of worthiness can take some getting used to. Your nervous system is learning how to feel comfortable receiving. That is a new experience for many people.

You are not charging for your time. You are charging for the transformation, relief, clarity, or experience your clients walk away with. You are also charging for the business that makes that transformation possible. Pricing supports the container that supports the client.

Many new entrepreneurs make a very understandable mistake when they price their first offers. They look at the one hour they spend with a client and believe the price should reflect only that hour. It seems straightforward. If a one-hour session costs one hundred dollars, that feels like a great exchange and a high wage. But the hour with the client is only one part of the service.

Every offering has a visible portion and an invisible portion. The visible part is what the client experiences. The invisible part is everything that makes that visible moment possible.

For a single session, there is often additional time and energy spent:

Preparing the space
Responding to messages
Setting up the equipment or materials
Creating notes or session plans
Purchasing and maintaining supplies
Marketing the service
Handling scheduling and rescheduling
Cleaning up afterward
Doing accounting and admin work
Continuing education and staying skilled in your craft
Regulating your own nervous system after emotional labor

When you add up the full picture, that one-hour offering is rarely just an hour. It might actually represent four to six hours of your time, energy, and resources. If you only charge for the visible part, the business will quietly drain you.

I learned this during the early years of running my massage business. I priced sessions based only on the hour of hands-on massage. I paid therapists a high percentage because I wanted to be generous and fair. What I did not calculate was the true cost to run the business. The rent. The insurance. The advertising. The laundry. The hours spent managing the schedule, paying bills, and leading a team. By the time all of that was covered, I was working constantly and earning less than I realized.

It was not a lack of money. It was a pricing structure that did not reflect reality. Once I understood the full energetic and practical investment behind each session, I changed the model. Pricing needed to honor the value of the experience and the business that made it possible.

That is the shift I want you to have from the beginning. You deserve to be supported by your work. When your pricing reflects the whole picture, your business becomes a source of nourishment instead of depletion.

When you are first starting, you are also learning what feels aligned. You are learning what the service asks of you. You are learning how much energy it takes and how confident you feel offering it. That is why pricing your first sample offer does not have to be perfect. It simply needs to feel doable and safe for you right now.

There are two simple ways to approach pricing in the beginning.

The first is to set a regular price that reflects where you want to go, and then offer a special rate while you build confidence. For example, you might set a regular rate of one hundred dollars but offer your first clients fifty percent off. After a few sessions, maybe the discount shifts to thirty percent. Then twenty percent. The regular price becomes the energetic anchor. The discount becomes the bridge while your nervous system adjusts to receiving more.

The second approach works beautifully with sample projects. You create one project with one specific price. That number exists only inside that experiment. When the project is complete, the next version has a new price. There is no explanation needed. You grew. Your confidence expanded. Your pricing expanded with you.

Both approaches honor you. Both approaches allow safety and growth. What matters is that the number feels aligned in your body.

You want a price that allows you to show up without resentment and without panic.

There is a misunderstanding in the healing and coaching world that higher pricing equals more success. People are encouraged to raise rates quickly. They are told to charge thousands before their nervous system is ready. If your body does not feel safe receiving that level of money, the energy collapses. You may avoid talking about your offer. You may quietly repel clients. The number might look good on the outside but feel very uncomfortable on the inside.

Your energy always tells the truth.

A price that is too high too fast can shut everything down.
A price that is too low can drain your energy and motivation.

Both come from fear, and both block momentum. Pricing becomes supportive when it feels like something you can stand inside with clarity and ease. When you can say the number without apology. When your body relaxes instead of braces.

Worthiness grows through experience. Confidence builds as you complete more projects, receive real feedback, and witness the impact you have on others. Every successful exchange expands your comfort with being compensated. Your price can evolve as your capacity increases.

Self-value is not a fixed identity. It shifts and grows as you do.

Let your early pricing be simple. Let it feel good enough to step forward. Your first prices are not your forever prices. They are your beginning. You do not need to wait until you feel fully worthy of higher numbers. You can grow into them. You can allow expansion to happen naturally.

Pricing is one of the ways you partner with your future. It allows your business to support you while you support others. It is not about proving your worth. Your worth is already here. Pricing is simply about creating a structure that sustains you as you bring your gifts into the world.

# Chapter Five: From Lone Wolf to Lighthouse

A business needs visibility to breathe. You can have a beautiful idea, a meaningful service, or a powerful offering, but if no one knows about it, it cannot reach the people who would love it. Visibility is not about forcing yourself into the spotlight. It is the gentle act of letting people know you exist. It is the flow of energy that signals, "I am here, I am available, and if this is meant for you, I would love to serve you." This is not selling. This is simply allowing yourself to be found.

Many women hesitate to share their new ideas because visibility can feel vulnerable. When something matters deeply to you, sharing it can bring up worries about being misunderstood, judged, or questioned. In the early stages of a soul-led business, your confidence is still growing. Your belief in your offer is forming. Your nervous system is learning what feels safe. So it's understandable that the idea of being seen brings up emotion. The body often equates visibility with risk, because it has been trained to seek safety in the familiar.

This is why many entrepreneurs find themselves procrastinating, endlessly preparing, or over-editing their ideas behind the scenes. They wait until their website looks perfect. They wait for the ideal brand photos. They wait until they feel "legit." But waiting to be perfect delays the support, clarity, and encouragement that visibility brings. If no one knows about your work, no one can say yes. The most talented people in the world can go unnoticed while others with average skill thrive simply because they are willing to let people know what they do.

The lone wolf pattern is a survival strategy many women have unconsciously inherited. It sounds like: "I'll just figure it out on my own," or "I don't want to bother anyone," or "Once I succeed, then I'll tell people." It may feel noble or independent, but business is a collaborative ecosystem. Growth happens faster and more joyfully when others are allowed to participate. Support, referrals, ideas, encouragement, and collaboration only arrive once people are aware that you're creating something.

Visibility doesn't have to be loud. It can be soft, gentle, and aligned with your nervous system. It can start in places that already feel safe. One woman wanted to test a coaching offer, but she felt too exposed to talk about it with her family. Instead, she posted inside an online metaphysical community where she felt understood. She offered a small package — three 45-minute sessions over three weeks. Her spots filled quickly. She gained confidence. She learned that she didn't need to make a big announcement to begin. She just needed to tell the right people first.

Visibility is a frequency. It is the energetic shift from "I'm working on it privately" to "I'm open and available." When you communicate that shift, support has room to appear. There are countless ways visibility can happen, and none of them require perfection. You can mention your project in a conversation. You can share a simple social post without branding or graphics. You can tell a friend, "If you know anyone who might enjoy this, feel free to connect us." This is not pressure - it is an invitation.

When you let yourself be seen, you activate momentum. People cannot engage with something they do not know exists. And often, others are excited to help simply because they admire someone following their curiosity and courage. They may not think to help unless you invite them. Not because they don't care, but because they don't realize their contribution would mean something. Allowing support is a skill. Many women are comfortable giving but uncomfortable receiving. They might instinctively decline help, minimize compliments, or downplay their work. But receiving is part of the creative loop. If you only give, the flow collapses.

Releasing the lone wolf identity is a powerful step in your evolution. You are not meant to do everything alone. No thriving business, spiritual mission, or visionary idea is carried by one person. When you share your work, you are setting a lighthouse out into the world - steady, warm, and inviting to the people who are already looking for what you offer. A lighthouse does not chase ships or wave a flag to get their attention. It simply shines. The ships who need it, notice.

Visibility is not proof you are ready. It is the process that makes you ready. You learn as you go because real feedback, real engagement, and real conversations show you what resonates. You do not need to know the whole plan to share your first step. You do not need certainty to let people know what you are creating. You only need the willingness to turn the light on.

This chapter is not about forcing yourself to be everywhere. It is about releasing the belief that you must stay hidden until you are successful. Success does not lead to visibility, visibility creates the pathway to success. When you allow your work to be seen, you allow the universe to respond to your desire. You allow opportunities to find you. You allow your business to grow in relationship with real humans.

You deserve to be witnessed in your beginning. You deserve to receive support before perfection. You deserve to feel that your voice, your ideas, and your offerings matter - right now. You are not meant to disappear into the background of your own dreams. You are meant to participate in them fully.

Every time you choose to share — even a small share — you strengthen your identity as someone who is here to contribute, create, and be seen. You are shifting from waiting to welcoming. You are stepping from isolation into connection. You are becoming a lighthouse, not by force, but by acknowledging your own glow.

That is how visibility becomes your frequency.
That is how momentum finds you.
That is how you Flow Forward.

# Chapter Six: The Art of Receiving

Receiving is one of the most underestimated business skills. It is often easier to give, serve, help, or support others than it is to allow money, recognition, or assistance to flow toward you. Many soul led entrepreneurs are incredible givers. They love helping others. But receiving can feel vulnerable because it requires openness. It requires letting others show up for you. It requires believing that you are worthy of support long before you feel fully ready or fully confident.

Receiving is what allows your business to nourish you. A business is meant to give as much as it asks of you. It is meant to support your life, your energy, your well being, and your dreams. You are not building something only to give and give until you are empty. You are building a living relationship with your business so that it can bless you as much as you bless others.

The body often has a much harder time receiving than the mind. This is because receiving requires trust. When someone pays you, compliments you, supports you, shares your work, or says yes to your offer, the nervous system can suddenly feel exposed. Old stories might rise to the surface. Stories about being selfish. Stories about being a burden. Stories about needing to prove worth before accepting anything in return. These are survival patterns, not personal failures.

Every human receives training in how to survive this world. Many women learn to survive by being the helper. The reliable one. The strong one who never needs anything. That strategy may have served you once, but in business it creates a pattern where you give value while blocking value from returning. That pattern leads to burnout. It leads to resentment. It leads to feeling invisible.

You deserve to feel supported. You deserve to receive payment that reflects the energy you offer. You deserve to let others uplift you. When you let yourself receive, your business becomes sustainable. When you allow money in, you gain resources to keep creating. When you accept praise, your confidence expands. When you welcome support, your nervous system relaxes. Receiving is not a luxury. It is a requirement for a thriving business.

Your business does not exist only to serve others. It exists to serve you too. It wants to be a channel that brings abundance into your life. That includes joy. That includes creative expression. That includes meaningful connection. And yes, that includes money. You are not here to struggle for your purpose. You are here to be resourced by it.

The universe responds to your willingness to receive. When you open your energy field to support, new opportunities begin to appear in forms you could not have planned. A stranger might share your post. A friend might refer a perfect client. A collaborator might show up out of nowhere. You do not need to know exactly how your success will unfold. You only need to remain open to the fact that life is trying to support you.

Receiving also includes the ability to allow feedback, ideas, and learning without shame. When you treat your business as a living experiment you become available for growth. You can refine. You can adjust. You can try again. You can learn through real interaction rather than imagining everything in your head. When you receive what the experience teaches you, you evolve faster than any course or certification could ever accomplish.

There is a consciousness to your business. It is not a to do list. It is a partnership. Your business is here to grow with you. It responds to your frequency. If your energy is in protection mode, your business cannot fully expand. If your energy is open and receptive, your business can begin sending support through people, resources, and aligned opportunities. You do not have to be the only force making everything happen. You are meant to be in co creation with something bigger than yourself.

Receiving is also a form of leadership. When you allow others to contribute to your vision, they feel inspired to rise with you. Your willingness to receive gives others permission to receive too. You become an example of ease, support, and aligned success. This is how we shift away from the old world model of sacrifice and struggle. When you receive fully, you create a new blueprint for others who thought they had to do everything alone.

This is your reminder. You do not have to earn the right to be supported. You do not need to wait for perfect readiness before you receive. You do not need to apologize for wanting more. You are allowed to receive support without over explaining. You are allowed to receive money without feeling guilty. You are allowed to receive encouragement without deflecting it. You are allowed to allow.

Receiving is a sacred skill. It is a nervous system skill. It is a prosperity skill. It is a manifestation skill. And it is one of the most important parts of entrepreneurship. You deserve to let it be easier. You deserve to feel held. You deserve to thrive inside the work that lights up your soul.

Let life give to you. Let people appreciate you. Let money flow to you. Let your business become a source of nourishment. You are here to co create with a universe that adores you and wants your dreams to come alive.

Receiving is how you Flow Forward.

# Chapter Seven: The Law of Circulation

Money is not the only form of wealth. Energy, attention, appreciation, ideas, joy, praise, and support are all currencies in the universe. They move in cycles. They like to flow. The Law of Circulation describes a simple truth: what you give, when aligned and resourced, returns to you multiplied. Not always from the same direction. Not always in the same form. But always in motion.

This law is always working, whether we understand it or not. When we participate consciously, we allow the flow to expand.

The universe is circular, not linear.
Nature is circular, not linear.
Your business is circular, not linear.

Everything you offer out is meant to continue moving until it flows back into your life in a new way. That might look like money. It might look like praise. It might look like a new opportunity, a client referral, a solution that appears out of nowhere, or a moment of deep personal expansion. The form changes, but the energy always returns.

The shift happens when you stop seeing giving as loss and begin seeing it as participation in a larger ecosystem.

## Giving Is Not the Same as Overgiving

Many women have already been trained as givers long before they ever start a business. They know how to care for others. They know how to show up. They know how to keep the needs of a community alive. But they often learned to give without receiving in return. They learned to give as a way to feel valuable or worthy. They learned to give as a survival strategy - to avoid rejection, criticism, or abandonment.

That kind of giving is not circulation. It is extraction.
You give and the energy disappears, leaving you depleted and unseen.

The Law of Circulation only activates when both ends of the exchange remain open.
Giving must feel supported.
Receiving must feel safe.

Otherwise, the circle collapses.

## The Overperformer Pattern

Overgiving and overperforming come from the same root: fear.

Fear that if you don't give enough, you won't be chosen.
Fear that if you don't do more, you won't be appreciated.
Fear that if you relax, you won't be valued.

The body learned this as protection long ago.
The nervous system still thinks it must earn belonging through effort.

When that old belief takes the lead, you spend energy faster than it flows back. You give beyond your capacity. You price below sustainability. You deliver more than you promised. You minimize your needs. You apologize for receiving. And even when abundance tries to reach you, the door is closed—because your identity is wrapped in being the strong one, the giver, the responsible one.

The universe may send the return flow, but if your receiving channels are blocked, the energy has nowhere to land.

## Closing the Circle

The circle closes when:

Receiving feels unsafe
Help feels like a threat to independence

Compliments are deflected
Money is refused or discounted
Support is turned down
Success is downplayed
Visibility is avoided

When you block receiving, you block return.
Instead of a circle, you create a drain.

You cannot pour out energy and expect to thrive if your system will not allow energy back in.

This is why your nervous system matters in business.
Your ability to receive is what keeps the flow alive.

Opening the Circle
The Law of Circulation activates when you do these things:

You give from fullness, not depletion
You receive without apology
You allow others to show up for you
You trust support instead of fearing it
You let your business nourish you
You believe your work has value
You say yes when money arrives

When both giving and receiving remain open, the energy multiplies.
It returns because there is space for it to land.

How the Return Flow Shows Up
We are trained to look only for money as proof of success. But the universe returns energy through many forms:

A client who gushes with appreciation
A new opportunity that seems to appear from nowhere

Being seen by someone who can help you
An idea that saves you hours of effort
Someone recommending your work without being asked
Unexpected resources or upgrades in your life
Feeling energized after serving
A collaboration invitation that expands your reach
Ease replacing struggle
A clear no that protects your alignment
A moment of inner confidence that changes everything

All of these are deposits. All of these are expansion.
All of these count as wealth.

Receiving generously allows the universe to keep giving generously.

Your Business Wants to Circulate
Your business is a living field. It wants:

Energy in
Energy out
Energy back

If you only serve and never receive, the business cannot breathe.
If you only receive and never serve, the business cannot grow.
The relationship thrives when both are honored.

Participation is the magic.
Exchange is the generator.
Flow is the currency.

A Simple Truth
You are not meant to give until empty.
You are meant to circulate energy through a system that supports you in return.

Instead of asking
How can I give more?

Ask
How can I allow support to return?

Every time you receive appreciation, payment, visibility, referrals, rest, joy, nourishment, or love, you are keeping the circle open. You are allowing abundance to come home.

And the more easefully you receive, the more confidently you can give again.
This is the Law of Circulation.
This is a sustainable business.
This is prosperity without struggle.

You are not here to only pour out.
You are here to participate in the flow.
You are here to expand the wealth of the world by letting it move through you.

Let yourself give with generosity.
Let yourself receive with grace.
Let yourself stay open.

Let circulation do what it always does, return everything you offer, multiplied in ways you could not plan.

This is how you Flow Forward.

# Chapter Eight: Embodiment

## Becoming the Frequency of What You Offer

There comes a moment on the entrepreneurial path where learning turns into living. This is embodiment. It is the shift from studying your message to becoming it. It is the moment when your offer stops being something you do and becomes something you are. You are no longer trying to convince anyone that your work matters. Your presence communicates that truth. Clients feel your grounded confidence long before they understand your full methodology. You become a tuning fork for the transformation you offer. Your business becomes a reflection of who you are becoming, not just what you know.

Embodiment is not perfection. It is presence. It is the daily practice of aligning your internal world with the external experience you are creating. You do not suddenly wake up embodied. You evolve into it through repetition, connection, nervous system safety, and lived experience. When your words and actions match the energy of your work, people trust you without needing proof.

Every new identity begins as a stretch. The moment you expand beyond the version of yourself that others are familiar with, doubt often rises. Imposter syndrome may appear. Your ego may question whether you belong in this new space. But imposter syndrome does not mean you are a fraud. It means you have entered the gap between who you have been and who you are growing into. The shakiness is not a warning. It is evidence of evolution.

I have walked this exact edge myself. I helped my first husband build a successful business. When I remarried, I helped my second husband grow and build his business as well. It always felt easy to support someone else in shining. When it came to my own business, I played small. I opened and ran Balancing Touch Massage, hired talented people, and provided for my two children on my own. Yet I found myself uncomfortable being seen as a leader. Some therapists I hired were older than me and I worried they would not see me as legitimate. I downplayed my role as the owner. Entrepreneurship felt natural to do, but very difficult to claim.

One day, a friend I met through the Abraham Hicks community said something that changed me forever. She said, “Sabrina, I had no idea you were such a successful businesswoman. You give the impression you are a stay-at-home parent. Yet here you are running a thriving business and supporting your family. That is incredible.” I remember feeling stunned. I knew I did not brag about my success, but I had never realized that I was actively hiding it. Her words flipped a switch inside me. It was the first time I allowed myself to see and embody that I was not just helping businesses thrive. I had built one. I was a successful entrepreneur.

This is embodiment. It is the moment you realize the identity you admired has already become you. It is the moment your nervous system allows you to take up the space you have rightfully earned.

Embodiment is about integrity. It is about living in relationship with what you offer rather than positioning yourself above it. If you support others in finding peace, you honor your own nervous system. If you help others create abundance, you are willing to increase your own capacity to receive. If you help others feel confident, you walk your own edges with tenderness and honesty. You do not need to be fully healed to help others heal. You do not need to be wealthy to hold space for abundance. You do not need to be fearless to lead. But you do need to be in participation with your values.

You can support your embodiment by surrounding yourself with the frequency you are growing into. Read books and listen to conversations that nourish your identity. Join communities that celebrate your expansion. Practice sharing your voice even when it feels new. Let your nervous system adapt to being a little more visible, expressed, and powerful each week. Let your life become the training ground where you embody the transformation you facilitate.

There will be days when you feel disconnected from your clarity. This does not mean you have lost your embodiment. It means you are integrating something important. The nervous system often escalates resistance right before a major expansion. When old patterns resurface, it is usually because a new level of embodiment is trying to establish itself. Instead of self judging or collapsing into old narratives, meet yourself with presence. The goal is never constant alignment. The goal is repair and return.

Embodiment is not a performance. It is permission. It is the permission to lead from your truth instead of your fear. It is the choice to believe in your becoming before others see the evidence. It is the softening into the knowing that you are allowed to grow publicly and imperfectly. You do not wait to embody abundance until your business is thriving. You embody abundance so your business can thrive. You do not wait to embody confidence until you have a full calendar. You embody confidence so clients feel safe entering your field. Your work becomes a lived invitation instead of a hopeful promise.

Ask yourself:

What identity am I practicing today?
How would I show up if I trusted that my future success is already done?
What would shift if I allowed myself to be seen for who I truly am rather than who I used to be?

The business you are creating is a mirror of the frequency you choose to stand in. Your voice, your pricing, your boundaries, and your presence communicate your embodiment long before your marketing does. You are not just here to talk about transformation. You are here to be the living proof that transformation is possible.

Let yourself grow into the future you are calling in. Let your nervous system catch up to your brilliance. Let your body trust that you can hold more. Embodiment is not an end state. It is a relationship with becoming. It is the moment your internal belief aligns with your external expression. It is the moment your purpose feels like home.

You are not here to only speak your magic. You are here to live it. And when you do, the world will feel the shift.

This is embodiment. This is leadership. This is Flow Forward.

# Chapter Nine: Flow Forward Blueprint

This chapter is your threshold moment. You have gathered the tools, the clarity, the vision, and the courage. Now everything in your system is humming with readiness. Your inner being has been preparing you for this exact moment. This is when thinking becomes becoming and desire becomes motion. This is where business shifts from imagination into activation. This is where Flow Forward becomes real.

**The Power of the Sample Offer**

Your first step into entrepreneurship does not need to be a grand launch. You do not need a website. You do not need a brand or perfect messaging or a business plan. You only need one simple thing. One small, real-world offer and one person who says yes.

A sample offer is like an appetizer. Small enough to feel doable. Light enough for your nervous system to say yes. Potent enough to open the door to everything that is coming next. You are not here to get it perfect. You are here to get it moving.

**The Language of Beginning**

There are many names for this first step.

Sample offer
Beta round
Pilot program
Test run
Intro offer
First version

All of these words mean the same thing. You are trying something for a short amount of time with a small number of people to see how it feels and what it teaches you.

There is no correct label. There is no official start. There is only movement.

A sample communicates simplicity. A beta communicates experimentation. A pilot communicates curiosity. A first version communicates activation.

Use any name that feels good. Change it every time if you want. The name is not the point. The experience is.

**Why Small Works**

Starting small dissolves pressure. It removes perfectionism from the driver's seat. It allows your nervous system to stay regulated as you become visible.

Instead of asking, what if I fail, you get to ask, what will I learn.

Small reveals what is aligned.

What lights you up
What drains you
What people respond to
What your body says yes to
Where your brilliance actually lives

You cannot think your way into clarity. You must move your way into clarity. Action reveals what imagination cannot.

## My Wild Wednesday Story

Before I opened my spa, I was not ready for a lease or large expenses. I simply wanted to work one day a week. So I walked around town asking business owners if they had a room I could rent.

Eventually, a martial arts studio owner showed me a large closet that was not being used. It was humble and perfect. He offered me a brilliant arrangement. I would only pay five dollars per appointment. If I had no clients, I paid nothing. If I worked, I earned. It was the ultimate low-risk experiment.

I made a simple flyer inside his gym.

Wild Wednesday
Sixty Minute Massage
Twenty Five Dollars

I paid him five dollars and I made twenty dollars per session. Yes, I undercharged. I was a new therapist and I felt happy with twenty dollars. Within weeks, I was fully booked every Wednesday. I worked there for about six months and discovered something important. I loved this industry. I loved working with people. I loved being in business. I felt ready to expand.

That tiny closet became the first stepping stone toward owning a thriving spa business. It did not need to be impressive. It just needed to begin.

## Time In Creates Confidence

Confidence does not come first. Confidence comes from being inside the work.

Time in the energy
Time in the visibility

Time in the receiving
Time in the doing

Your nervous system learns. I am safe to serve. I am safe to shine. This is identity building. This is embodiment through action. This is how your business becomes real.

**What If No One Buys**

This is the fear that stops most dreams. But here is the truth. If no one buys, you are not failing.

You are learning what the offer wants.
You are learning how people understand it.
You are learning where alignment lives.

You are strengthening your courage.
You are practicing visibility.
You are preparing your field for money.

Every experiment is successful when the goal is information.

## Your Offer Is a Conversation with Life

Your business is not a task. It is a living field. It is communicating with you. You can ask your offer.

What is the simplest version of you
Who are the first people ready to say yes
Where do you want to be shared
What do you want to teach me

Let the answers come through intuition, synchronicity, and the next obvious step. Your business wants to collaborate with you. It wants to grow with you. It wants you to listen.

## The Flow Forward Formula

One idea
One price
One time frame
One invitation
One yes

Everything else is refinement.

Your Tiny Yes Is Sacred

Start small and you learn.
Start small and you build confidence.
Start small and you become the entrepreneur.
Start small and you flow forward.

Every business begins as a whisper.
Every empire begins with a spark.
Every breakthrough begins with the courage to begin.

Your future self is already celebrating.
She knows how much this chapter unlocks.

Start small.
Start simple.
Start now.

Let movement happen.
Let people notice.
Let support arrive.
Let momentum build.

This is your yes moment.
Flow forward. The path is already rising to meet you.

# Chapter Ten: Let Momentum Lead

The first offer is a beginning. It is the activation point. It tells life that you are ready to participate in your desires. But what happens after that beginning is just as important. This is where identity begins to strengthen. This is where the universe shows you what is possible. This is where momentum becomes your ally.

Your first offer is not the finish line. It is the ignition. It is the moment the engine turns on. When energy is already in motion, everything becomes easier. New ideas come faster. Confidence builds naturally. The mind stops trying to predict every outcome because now you have lived experience guiding you.

The most common mistake people make after a successful sample offer is thinking they need to take a huge leap to prove they are legitimate. They believe they must suddenly perfect their brand, expand their services, raise their prices, ramp up marketing, or lock in a long-term commitment. That pressure interrupts flow.

Momentum does not ask you to go bigger. Momentum asks you to keep going.

The beauty of your early stage is how flexible you still are. You are learning what works, what feels aligned, what brings you joy, and how you want to show up. You do not need to have a strategy yet. You simply need to listen to the feedback from what is already happening.

Ask yourself these gentle questions

What felt the easiest
What brought me the most joy
Where did I feel most like myself

What part required extra energy or support
What do I want to repeat
What do I want to refine

Do not rush to change everything. Let your experience teach you. Your nervous system is learning that being seen is safe and being paid is supportive. You are collecting evidence that your gifts belong in the world.

Let your second offer be just as simple. It might be the same service again. It might be a small adjustment. It might be a clearer version of what you already shared. Your work will evolve with each repetition but repetition is foundational to mastery.

Momentum grows through consistency, not complexity.

Your second and third offers are less about invention and more about refinement. You are getting to know your business the same way you get to know a relationship. You learn how it communicates. You learn what feels energizing. You learn where your unique brilliance lives.

This stage is where your confidence multiplies. You begin to see yourself through the eyes of the people you help. You recognize the transformation you create. You realize you are not imagining your value. People are responding to it.

When doubt appears, remember this truth: doubt often visits right after a success. It is a protective instinct. The nervous system sometimes worries that if something went well, the next step might be risky. Your job is not to overpower the doubt. Your job is to reassure the part of you that is still learning safety.

Tell yourself: we can move slowly. We can take one step. We are allowed to keep going.

Momentum does not always look fast. Sometimes it looks steady. Sometimes it looks gentle. What matters is that you do not shut the door you just bravely opened.

Let momentum lead you to the next aligned step

It could be inviting feedback from your clients
It could be sharing your offer again with clearer language
It could be adding something small that feels exciting
It could be practicing saying your price out loud with confidence
It could be allowing someone to refer a friend

Each choice becomes another vote for the future you are creating.

You are not required to leap into a big business. You are invited to flow forward into a sustainable one. Each step becomes easier because the path is now familiar.

You are building a body of evidence that says you are capable. You are building a new identity rooted in self trust. You are building a business that grows at the speed of alignment.

Let momentum lead. Let the next step reveal itself. Let gentle action build the bridge. Let your confidence rise from the inside out.

You already began. That is the hardest part. Now you get to stay in the game and discover what wants to unfold next.

Your job is not to push. Your job is to participate. Your job is to stay willing. Your job is to keep saying yes to the version of you who knows she is meant to thrive.

The path is open. The energy is flowing. Your future success is already in motion.

All you need to do is keep going.

**Your Yes Changes Everything**

You began this journey with an idea - a spark. Something inside you whispered that there is more for you. More creativity. More alignment. More joy. More expression. More ways to serve and be seen.

And now, you have already become someone different.

You are no longer someone who only *dreams* about a business.
You are someone who takes aligned action.
You are someone who partners with your inner being.
You are someone who knows that movement creates momentum.

Entrepreneurship is not a destination. It is a relationship - with yourself, with your creativity, with the universe. Each step you take strengthens your identity as a creator. Each offer you share strengthens your belief in your gifts. Each experience, whether wildly successful or simply informative, becomes a stepping stone to the business that is meant for you.

You have already proven something powerful to yourself:
You are safe to begin.
You are capable of learning as you go.
You are worthy of being supported.
You are allowed to grow at the speed of alignment.

You do not need to know where all of this leads to trust that you are on your path. Your job is not to see the whole map, only to follow the next clear step. Flow Forward is not about rushing or pushing. It is about allowing. Listening. Taking one small step in curiosity and confidence, again and again, until your business reveals its potential.

Some days you will feel unstoppable. Some days you will feel unsure. But doubt does not mean you are off track. It means you are expanding. You are building a new identity. You are activating new levels of self-trust.

Remember this:
Momentum does not come from a giant leap. It comes from saying yes to the smallest invitation.

Yes, I will try.
Yes, I will share.
Yes, I will receive.
Yes, I will keep going.

Your business is already awake. It has a pulse. It has a personality. It has a place in this world. And it chose you, because you are the perfect person to bring it to life.

So breathe. Smile. Celebrate.
You have begun, and that is everything.

This is your new origin story.

Flow Forward

# Flow Forward Workbook

Practical Tools to Move Your Idea Into Motion

This workbook is a guided flow. Follow one step at a time. You are not building a full business. You are starting a friendly experiment that lets you gather real-world information. The goal is movement, not mastery.

Every prompt is designed to help you enter the current of your new identity as someone who takes action on what feels alive.

Let’s begin.

## Chapter One Worksheet
## The Experiment Mindset

Entrepreneurship begins as curiosity, not certainty.
This page helps you explore what is calling you forward without pressure or perfection.

What idea or project has been circling in your mind lately?

What excites you about this idea?

What fears or worries appear when you think about beginning?

Where do you feel this idea in your body?

What would be worth discovering, even if the idea changes later?

What parts of entrepreneurship do you already know you enjoy?

What parts feel new or uncertain, but maybe interesting to explore?

What might you learn about yourself if you simply try?

How does it feel to imagine starting small instead of all at once?

What is one reason you want to give this idea a chance to exist?

Give yourself one sentence of permission to begin lightly.

**Ask-firmations for Chapter One**

Why is it safe for me to begin before I feel ready?

Why is curiosity enough to start?

Why do I get to explore without committing forever?

Why am I allowed to learn as I go?

Why is my idea worthy of being tested in the real world?

Why does taking a small step create big clarity for me?

Why is flow already preparing the support I will need?

Why does trying something new build trust in myself?

Why is it exciting to let the experience teach me?

Why am I so good at finding what feels aligned?

Why is this business experiment already working out for me?

Why does starting small open the door to unexpected success?

Why do I naturally follow the ideas that light me up?

Why does momentum love meeting me the moment I move?

## Chapter Two Worksheet
## Start With One Simple Offer

Movement creates clarity.
This page helps you simplify your idea into a small, joyful experiment.

What idea feels light enough to try first?

Why does this idea feel like a match for right now?

What is the simplest version of this idea that I can offer?

What would I love someone to walk away with?

Who is the kind of person I imagine saying yes?

Where do I feel excitement in my body when I think about sharing this?

How can I keep this playful instead of perfect?

What is one small step I can take this week to bring this offer into motion?

What feels optional that I can let go of?

What feels essential that I want to include?

If I treated this as a friendly experiment, how would that change the energy?

## Ask-firmations for Chapter Two

Why is one simple offer enough to activate momentum?

Why does the universe respond the moment I move?

Why is clarity waiting for me on the other side of action?

Why is it safe to test my idea in a small way first?

Why do the right people notice when I take a brave step?

Why am I so good at starting lightly?

Why does my body already know what wants to happen next?

Why does keeping it simple feel so aligned for me?

Why do small beginnings lead to big possibilities in my life?

Why am I allowed to learn through doing, not planning?

Why is my simple offer already opening doors for me?

Why does momentum love meeting me halfway?

Why do I trust the idea that feels alive right now?

Why is one yes all I need to begin?

Why does the next step always reveal itself as soon as I start?

## Chapter Three Worksheet
## Protect Your Energy When You Begin

This beginning is a tender phase.
Your nervous system is learning that it is safe to try.
These prompts help you stay in your own lane and move at a pace that feels supportive.

Where do I feel the most safety and encouragement to share my beginning?

Who are the people I feel comfortable inviting into this first version?

Who might I wait to tell until I feel more grounded and confident?

What boundaries support my energy as I experiment?

Where does my body feel tense or protective when I think about being visible?

What reassurance or comfort does that part of me need?

How can I keep this experience small enough that I stay in motion?

What would help me soothe my nervous system this week as I take a step?

Where do I feel proud of myself already?

**Ask-firmations for Chapter Three**

Why is it safe for me to try something new even if no one else understands yet?

Why does starting gently support my confidence?

Why do I attract support from the right people at the right time?

Why do I listen to my body when it asks for safety?

Why is my peace more important than proving anything?

Why do I trust myself to move slowly and still succeed?

Why does protecting my energy help my business grow stronger?

Why am I allowed to share my beginnings only where I feel seen?

Why do the people meant for me always find me?

Why do I feel more confident every time I honor my needs?

Why is it powerful to let my dream grow roots before I make it big?

Why does my nervous system relax more each time I take a small step?

Why do I feel more supported than I ever realized?

Why is it enough to begin quietly and confidently?

## Chapter Four Worksheet
## The Energy of Pricing

Pricing is not just a number.
It is a conversation between your worth, your energy, and your nervous system.
These prompts help you choose a price that supports you and your client.

What number feels safe and doable for this first version?

How does my body respond when I say this price out loud?

What would make this exchange feel fair and nourishing to me?

What costs of time, energy, and preparation need to be included in my price?

What price helps me show up without resentment?

If I offered a temporary rate for this experiment, what would that look like?

How can I practice saying this price with clarity and calm?

Where do I still feel uncomfortable receiving money?

What belief about my value is ready to evolve?

**Ask-firmations for Chapter Four**

Why is it safe for me to charge for the transformation I provide?

Why do I deserve to be supported as I support others?

Why does receiving money make space for me to give more fully?

Why do aligned clients happily pay the price that feels right for me?

Why am I worthy of choosing a price that nourishes me?

Why does clarity in pricing make everything easier?

Why am I allowed to increase my pricing as my confidence grows?

Why does my value expand every time I say my price out loud?

Why do I feel more powerful each time I choose supportive pricing?

Why does the universe celebrate every time I receive?

Why do I trust that the right clients appreciate what I offer?

Why am I a match for abundance that feels peaceful and steady?

Why is my work worthy of being compensated beautifully?

Why do I feel more confident around money every day?

Chapter Five Worksheet
From Lone Wolf to Lighthouse

Visibility is not loud.
It is simply letting the right people know you exist.
These prompts support soft visibility that feels safe and aligned.

Where do I feel most comfortable sharing my offer at this stage?

Who already feels supportive, curious, or encouraging about what I'm creating?

What simple way can I let someone know I am available?

How can I share without overexplaining or apologizing?

What feels like an easy first visibility step?

Where do I feel energized when I imagine being seen?

If someone offered help or connection, how could I allow myself to receive it?

What is one way I can shine a little bit brighter this week?

**Ask-firmations for Chapter Five**

Why is it safe for me to be seen in my beginning?

Why do people love discovering what I have to offer?

Why am I so good at letting the right people find me?

Why does sharing my work feel easier every time I do it?

Why does visibility create opportunities that are meant for me?

Why am I worthy of support, referrals, and encouragement?

Why do others feel inspired when I shine my light?

Why does my presence naturally attract aligned clients?

Why is it so easy for me to be visible in places where I feel safe?

Why do I feel confident letting people know I'm available?

Why do opportunities show up when I take small visibility steps?

Why am I supported in every direction as I grow?

Why is simply being myself the most magnetic visibility strategy?

## Chapter Six Worksheet
## The Art of Receiving

Receiving is how your business gets to take care of you.
These prompts help you allow support, money, appreciation, and opportunity to land in your life.

Where do I feel resistance or discomfort when someone wants to support me?

What story have I carried about needing to earn everything I receive?

What would feel easier if I allowed more support in my business?

What new belief about receiving wants to take root?

How does my body feel when I imagine being paid with ease?

Where in my life do I already receive well?

What is one small way I can let someone help me this week?

What am I willing to stop apologizing for or minimizing?

How might my business thrive if I opened the door to more nourishment?

**Ask-firmations for Chapter Six**

Why is it safe for me to receive fully and freely?

Why do I deserve to be supported in all the ways I support others?

Why does money feel welcome in my world?

Why do people love paying me for the value I provide?

Why am I allowed to receive before I feel perfectly ready?

Why does my nervous system relax when I let abundance in?

Why do compliments and praise feel easier to receive every day?

Why does receiving make my work more sustainable and joyful?

Why am I worthy of generosity, help, and celebration?

Why do aligned opportunities appear when I stay open?

Why does my value grow every time I allow myself to receive?

Why is being supported my new normal?

Why do I trust the flow that is trying to support me?

Why does receiving amplify the impact I am here to make?

## Chapter Seven Worksheet
## The Law of Circulation

Energy is meant to move.
When you give from fullness and receive with openness, abundance returns to you in many forms.
These prompts help you keep the circle flowing.

Where in my life or business do I give more than I receive?

Where do I feel nourished and energized by my giving?

How do I know when giving begins to drain me?

What does supportive, reciprocal exchange look like for me?

What would help me receive the return flow with more ease?

Where am I learning that my needs matter too?

How can I let others contribute to me without guilt?

What is one way I can honor the balance of giving and receiving this week?

Where do I already see evidence of return flow in my life?

**Ask-firmations for Chapter Seven**

Why is it safe for me to keep the circle open?

Why do I deserve to receive in the same flow that I give?

Why does abundance return to me multiplied?

Why do I feel energized when exchange is balanced?

Why does my generosity grow stronger when I am nourished too?

Why do I attract opportunities that support my expansion?

Why am I allowed to give only when it feels aligned?

Why do I trust that what I offer always comes back to me?

Why do appreciation, support, and prosperity flow toward me easily?

Why does my nervous system feel safe with receiving as much as I give?

Why is circulation my natural state?

Why does the universe delight in giving back to me?

Why do I feel more prosperous the more open I become?

## Chapter Eight Worksheet
## Embodiment: Becoming the Frequency of What You Offer

You are growing into the identity you have already chosen. Embodiment is the practice of living your message in real time, gently, honestly, and at the pace your nervous system can hold.

Where do I already feel like the version of myself who succeeds in this business?

How does my future, fully embodied self move through her day?

What choices help me feel more like the entrepreneur I am becoming?

Where do I still feel like I'm practicing a new identity?

What area of my business would benefit from more presence instead of more pressure?

What supportive actions remind my nervous system that I belong here?

How can I show myself that it's safe to take up space with my gifts?

What is evidence from this week that I am already embodying a new frequency?

What would shift if I trusted that who I am is enough right now?

**Ask-firmations for Chapter Eight**

Why is it safe to grow into who I am becoming?

Why do I already feel the identity of a successful entrepreneur taking root?

Why does alignment make my business more magnetic than perfection ever could?

Why do people feel the truth of my work through my presence?

Why am I worthy of being seen in my evolution, not just my completion?

Why do I trust that my message becomes more powerful as I live it?

Why does confidence expand each time I show up authentically?

Why is my future self proud of the choices I'm making today?

Why do I naturally embody the transformation I offer others?

Why does my energy speak louder than any strategy?

Why do opportunities flow to me when I stand in my truth?

Why is my becoming inevitable?

Chapter Ten Worksheet
Let Momentum Lead

Your business is already in motion.
Momentum grows when you take the next aligned step - without rushing, forcing, or trying to prove anything.
Let what is working guide you forward.

What felt surprisingly easy in my first offer?

What part of the experience brought me joy?

Where did my energy feel the strongest?

What did I learn that will help me refine my next offer?

What do I want to repeat because it felt aligned?

What do I want to adjust because it drained me?

What is the next small step that feels clear and doable?

What support or structure would help me stay consistent?

Where am I already seeing evidence that momentum is here?

**Ask-firmations for Chapter Ten**

Why does every step I take make the next one easier?

Why is momentum already working in my favor?

Why do small actions lead to big clarity for me?

Why do aligned opportunities show up when I stay in motion?

Why do I trust myself to keep going?

Why does the universe meet me halfway the moment I say yes?

Why is it safe to grow steadily and sustainably?

Why does momentum accelerate when I stay present?

Why is continuing easier than starting over?

Why am I proud of the progress I've already made?

Why does my confidence rise every time I take the next step?

Why is the path ahead opening up beautifully for me?

**Momentum Map Summary**
Your Flow Forward Checklist

This is your reminder that business begins with movement, not magnitude.
Return to this map anytime you feel unsure of your next step.

One idea that feels alive right now.

One simple offer that is easy to share.

One aligned price that feels supportive.

One short time frame that keeps it playful.

One safe place to share it.

One person to directly invite.

One yes to activate momentum.

One reflection to guide your next step.

You do not have to leap.
You only have to move.
Momentum will meet you.

Coming Next in The Soul Business Series…

## **Stay With It**

You started. You took action. You proved to yourself that this business is real. And now you have entered the normal part of entrepreneurship where the excitement fades and the doubts show up. Nothing has gone wrong. Most people quit here because they think that dip means they are not good enough, or the idea is not working. Stay With It is about learning how to keep going even when things feel slow or uncertain. You will build confidence through consistency. You will learn how to stay focused on what works, manage the discomfort, and continue moving forward. This is how you create results that last. This is how you become someone who follows through. This is what successful entrepreneurs do. They stay with it.

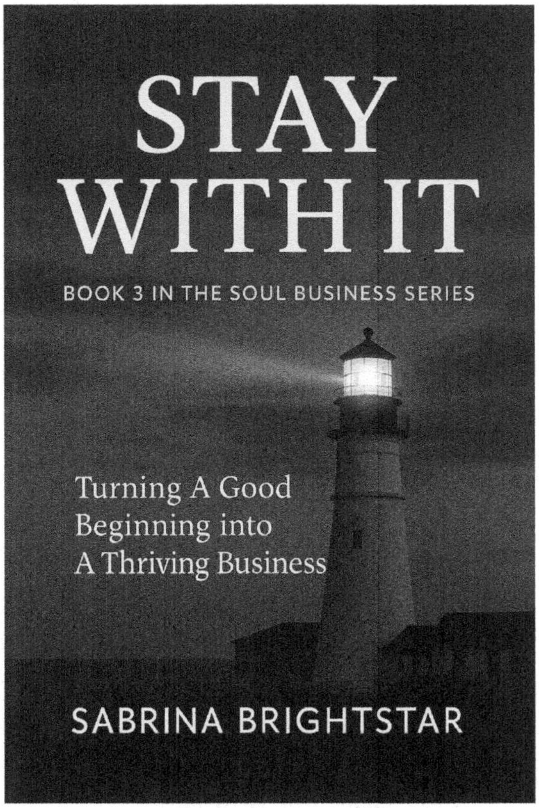

More E.books from Sabrina Brightstar

**Eyes of Discernment**
*From Seeking to Sovereignty*

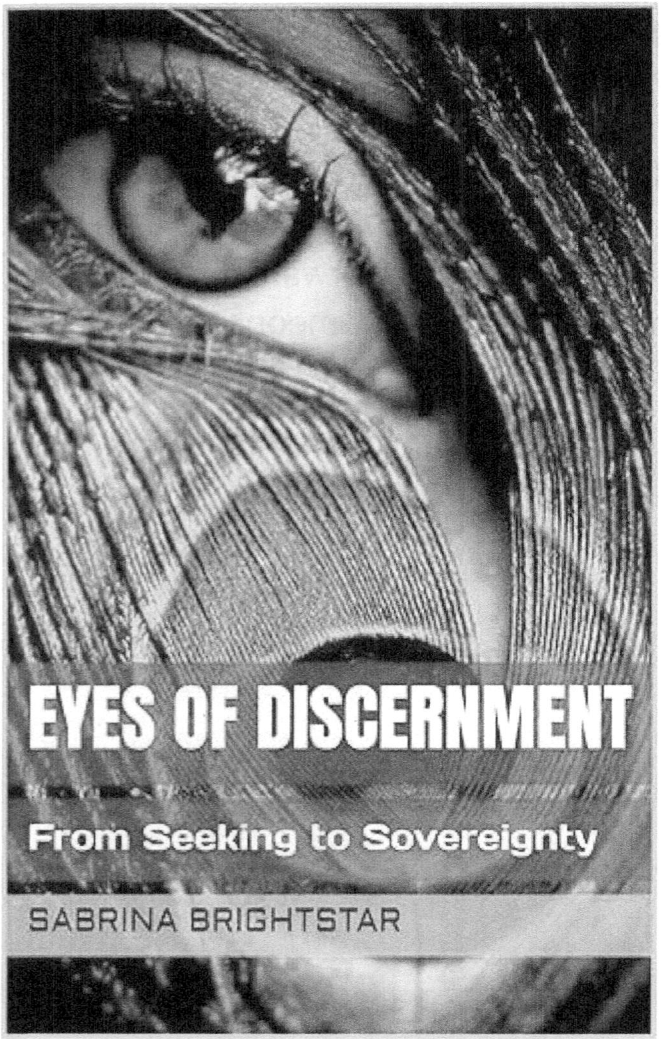


There comes a point in every spiritual seeker's journey where something shifts.

You have the language. You have the practice.
You've healed, learned, awakened - yet something still feels slightly off.

**Eyes of Discernment** is written for that moment.

This book bridges the gap between doing the work and **trusting yourself as the work**. It explores what happens when growth is no longer measured by how much you learn but by how deeply you listen to your own inner authority.

Inside, you'll explore themes such as:

- How spiritual devotion can quietly become spiritual obedience
- The difference between honoring a teacher and giving away your power
- Why some healing spaces feed dependency instead of expansion
- How to recognize influence that pulls you out of your own knowing
- The nervous system's role in sovereignty and discernment
- How to shift from "What do they say" to "What do I sense"

This book offers clarity for those who feel:

- Overloaded by advice and external guidance
- Confused about conflicting teachings in the spiritual world
- Pressured to perform healing rather than embody it
- Called to step into leadership instead of lifelong studenthood

Each chapter includes reflective prompts to recalibrate your inner compass — not toward a new system or authority — but back to the **truth already living inside you**.

**Eyes of Discernment** is not about rejecting guidance.
It is about **no longer abandoning yourself** inside it.

If you are ready to shift from seeker to sovereign — this book is your invitation.

**Awaken the Rebel Within**
*Re-Write HerStory*

You weren't born to fit into the story you were given.
You were born to **rewrite it**.

**Awaken the Rebel Within** is a guide for women who feel the growing pressure of their own truth — the ones who know they are done shrinking, done performing, and done waiting for permission to be who they really are.

This book will help you:

- Break free from the internalized rules that were never yours
- Reclaim your voice, intuition, and inner authority
- Transform sensitivity into sovereignty
- Rewrite limiting narratives rooted in patriarchy and survival
- Activate your divine feminine power and live uncensored

Through compassionate reflection and powerful writing exercises, you'll unravel the old programming and awaken the bold, intuitive leader within — the version of you who doesn't apologize for her power.

This isn't rebellion for rebellion's sake.
This is sacred rebellion — the kind that comes from remembering who you truly are.

If you are ready to rise, take up space, and write a new story for your life… your time has come.

**The Frequency of Relationships**
Love, Connection, and Sacred Union in the New Earth
Guided Workbook for Conscious Love, Soul Aligned Partnership, and Inner Union

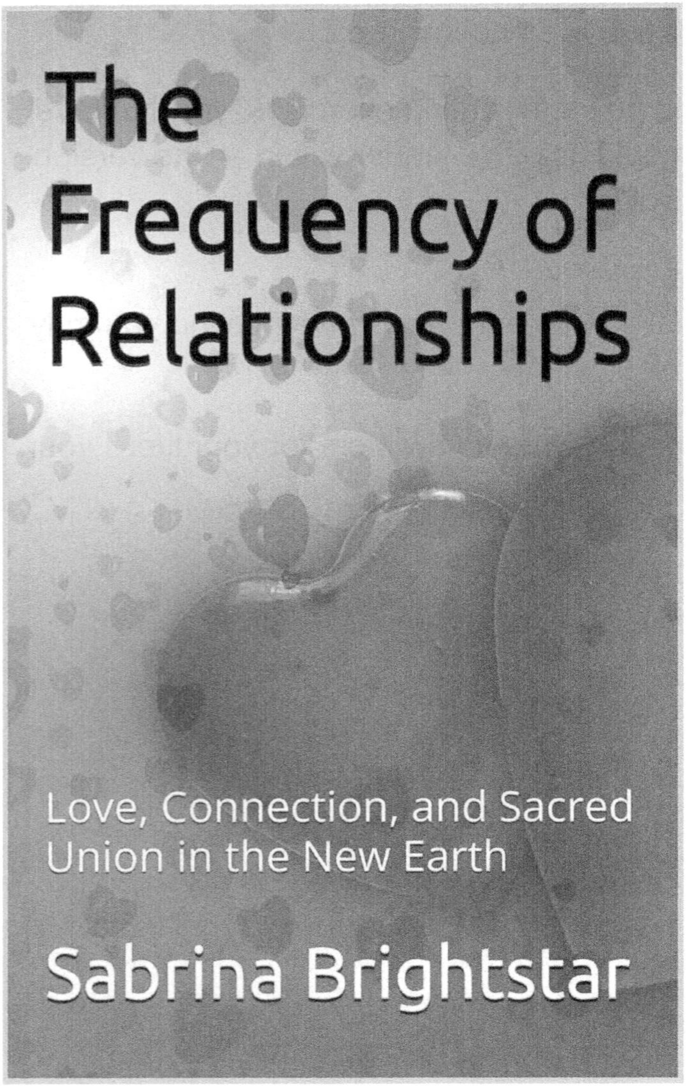


The Frequency of Relationships is a guided workbook and companion for anyone ready to experience love in a completely new way. This journey supports you in releasing outdated patterns, healing emotional imprints, and reconnecting with your Inner Being as the foundation of all healthy connections. Through powerful journaling prompts, self reflection, and AI assisted guidance, you will explore relationships from the lens of truth, sovereignty, and self worth.

Discover how to attract soul aligned partnerships, deepen existing relationships, and embody the frequency of sacred union. This workbook reminds you that the relationship you have with yourself sets the tone for every relationship in your life. When you anchor into self love and inner alignment, you naturally call in people who honor the real you.

This is your invitation to experience love that feels mutual, energizing, and aligned with your highest expression. A new template of connection is here. You are ready to receive it.

Made in the USA
Coppell, TX
04 November 2026

11286708R00046